DONALD J. TRUMP

The Tyrant in the White House

by Dr. Ray C. Minor

RoseDog Books

PITTSBURGH, PENNSYLVANIA 15238

RoseDog Books
585 Alpha Drive
Suite 103
Pittsburgh, PA 15238
Visit our website at *www.rosedogbookstore.com*

ISBN: 978-1-6442-6711-0
eISBN: 978-1-6442-6734-9

INTRODUCTION

I recently published my thoughts on Obama and his administrations in *Reflections on President Barack Obama. The first president of color of the United States* (2018). I had mixed emotions about Obama in the sense that he was a special case and had the capacity to be great but fell short because of partisan politics and his leadership style. In Trump we have a president who is all personality, very limited intellectually and morally deficient. So, without skipping a beat in writing on American politics, I focused squarely on Trump and his band of misfits. Trump poses a threat to democracy in general and to America in particular. A democratic president must first value the people of whom he is sworn to serve and defend. Secondly, especially in America, the president must honor and uphold the US constitution. Finally, the president must respect in word and deed the rule of law. Character and fitness to serve in the highest public office in the land are very important too but can be tolerated to the extent of the president not violating any laws. It just becomes embarrassing and nuisance behavior until laws are broken. Never in my life have I experienced or witnessed a US president with the personality, behavior and intelligence of Trump. My comments on Trump, his Administration and his business associates capture my thoughts as they occurred on or around the dates indicated. In essence, my comments are pleas for the checks and balances system to work, the restoration of democratic institutions, respect for the rule of law, honor for the US Constitution and the redemption of the American spirit.

MOST DESPICABLE PRESIDENT

In less than 8 months Donald J. Trump has proven to be the most despicable president imaginable. The majority of voters in the 2016 Election knew him to be unfit and unqualified for the highest public office in the land and therefore cast their votes for Hillary Clinton. A majority of the Electoral College's misfits handpicked Trump for the presidency. From day one, Trump began to illustrate his anti-democratic, anti-people and anti-world tendencies by appointing cabinet members and executive staff whose goals were to dismantle government-department by department and write and rewrite policies detrimental to people of color especially Muslims. He initiated an alleged unconstitutional travel ban on Muslims, attempted to repeal and replace Obamacare with the possibility of leaving 15-27 million citizens without any healthcare coverage.

In the meantime, Trump continued to kowtow or otherwise sheepishly bow down to Russian President Vladimir Putin. Trump refused to completely separate himself from his business interests and instead continued to promote his business interests at every presidential opportunity including meetings with foreign dignitaries. To demonstrate his ardent defiance and disdain for established protocol and respect for governmental officials, he appointed his daughter and son-in-law as confidants in the White House. Neither had any government experience. Trump further demonstrated his repudiation for status quo by appointing as senior advisors and officials, persons known as white supremacists and Neo-Nazis. This president even had the audacity to pull the US out of the Paris Agreement (climate change agreement) signed by Obama in 2016. Trump's disposition as a 10 years old can be seen in his babbling and bullying tweets to anyone who does not follow his edits or those who critique his misstatements, falsehoods, inappropriate remarks and bad behaviors. As I write, this bumbling president has the US on the brink of nuclear war with North Korea. I first predicted that his presidency would end in 18 months from his swearing in ceremony. Now I believe it may end within 12 months of that date. This president is the gravest threat to America's national security.

HELL NO

As a candidate during the 2016 Elections Donald J. Trump asked African Americans "What the hell do you have to lose?" (Meaning if African Americans voted for him. In reference to their reluctance to vote for him.) My response during the time was life, liberty and pursuit of happiness! A more important question, why would any rational voter vote for him? He has more than once demonstrated his childlike speech and behavior. Further, his intelligence level appeared to be below average. His temperament appeared immature and unstable. His language was usually lewd and vulgar. His demeanor appeared to be eccentric and narcissistic. So, Hell No, you will not get my vote!

GOOD PEOPLE ON BOTH SIDES

A most despicable president is Donald J. Trump. On yesterday Trump attempted to clarify his statement regarding the white supremacy disturbance in Charlottesville, VA that occurred over the weekend. His initial statement was there were many sides to blame for the melee. After much pushback from media, politicians and others, Trump made a second statement denouncing white supremacy, white nationalists and Neo-Nazis. Then on yesterday, Trump made the most despicable statement of all when he said "the white nationalists were treated unfairly by the media and that they were peacefully protesting the removal of the Robert E. Lee statue." And that "the white nationalists had a permit to demonstrate and the other group did not." And that "there were good people on both sides." He took a bold stand for white supremacy rather than denouncing hate groups in America. If any rational person doubted whether Trump was a bigoted racist, this stance made it crystal clear. Except for a handful of Republicans, a few business leaders and a host of Democrats, Trump's remarks were not publicly denounced by other politicians and business leaders. Where were the Republicans who hounded Barack Obama at every turn? Trump has proven beyond doubt that he is incapable of carrying out his duties as president. So why aren't Republicans joining Democrats in calling for his impeachment? The political clouds become more dark and ominous each day Trump remains in office.

Back on Charlottesville, there were more than 100 or so white nationalists and Neo-Nazis and KKK members marching with torches through the streets of Charlottesville last Friday shouting the hate filled slogan "Blood and soil". On the next day these groups were engaged in street fights with counter protesters. One of the white nationalists/Neo-Nazis drove his car into a crowd of protesters killing Heather Heyer and injuring 20 others. Two state police officers also lost their lives after tracking the event by helicopter in a crash later that day. No Mr. Trump, protector of white supremacists, these events were not peaceful or nonviolent. The most honorable thing for this president to do is to resign in shame.

IMPEACHMENT

The Trumpster got rid of Steve Bannon, white nationalist and racist, last week. Great! Now it's time for Congress to boot his ass out the door! Impeachment is the order of the day! Where are the Republicans who hounded Obama for 8 years? In a time when the worst president in US history sits in the Oval Office, these same Republican hounds sit in their kennels without barking and are in no mood to hunt down this president for waste, fraud and abuse. The Trump administration is overflowing with scandals. Donald Trump has committed another unconscionable act in the wake of the Charlottesville white supremacy melee. Trump pardoned one of the worst white nationalist public servants in US history, former Sherriff Joe Arpaio of Arizona. This despicable former Sheriff and his officers routinely racially profiled Latino drivers and passengers and stopped them under the pretext of enforcing immigration laws. However, to some in Trump's inner circle credit, he did remove another devout white nationalist/Neo-Nazi, Sebastian Gorka, from his executive staff. It appears that Trump continues to obstruct justice by interfering with those who may have bearing on the Russian investigation. His latest attempt since firing James Comey, former FBI

Director, is calling senators to not support a bill protecting the current FBI Director and Bob Mueller, special prosecutor, from firing. Why haven't the raging Republicans who persistently hounded Obama reigned in a known charlatan in the person of Donald Trump? This vile personality has signed an edit and sent it to the Secretary of Defense to purge the military of transgender soldiers. This Trump guy has consistently lacked a basic understanding of law, policy, history and ethics. Some even question his mental stability. He is the greatest threat to US national security. Impeach this president today! Tomorrow may be too late! If Congress does not initiate and effect impeachment then all of the members who oppose should be thrown out of office ASAP.

On yesterday Trump issued an order overturning or eliminating DACA in six months affecting 800,000 young persons primarily of color. He stated that he "loves these people but wants them to enter the country legally." Racism and racial hatred are reproduced in every generation. Every generation has its national racist leader or bigot. Trump is carrying the racist/bigoted torch for this time. We should not be surprised by his DACA decision given his attempt to ban Muslims and his tireless rant about building a wall between Mexico and the US. If his intensions were honorable and pure he would be just as aggressive in building a wall between US and Canada. My guess is that he wants only to bar people of color, particular ethnicities and certain religious backgrounds. Further, it appears that his ultimate goals include eradicating the legacy of Obama and the creation of a white state. This 45th president will be remembered as one of the worst US presidents in history.

KIM JONG-UN

On yesterday, the person who sits in the Oval Office spoke at the UN calling the President of North Korea, Kim Jong-un "a rocket man on a suicide mission". Trump was referring to Jong-un's penchant for displaying and launching rockets. Trump declared that he will totally destroy North Korea. As if Trump was vying for the most despicable president's title in US history, a title he has already earned. To minimize the International damage that Trump is capable of, Congress should initiate and expedite impeachment proceedings while his Cabinet simultaneously declare him incompetent and remove him from office. At the same time, the National Security Council should block him at all costs from executing nuclear codes. Trump should be placed in a straight-jacket and padded cell if necessary. Why don't the Congressmen who pursued President Obama from every angle on falsehoods and innuendoes confront and remove this crooked, unethical and psychopathic individual from public office? May God bless America!

SOB

Trump spoke in my home state of Alabama while campaigning for a senate candidate with whom I am casually familiar- Luther Strange. Like a hound dog with diarrhea Trump keeps pooping all over the place. He cannot stop! One of his latest attacks was on Colin Kaepernick, an NFL football player who exercised his constitutional right not to solute the Pledge of Allegiance to the Flag at the beginning of a football game. He instead kneeled on one knee and inspired a few other players to do the same. They were in fact protesting the injustices people of color face in the US especially police shootings of black males.

Now, Trump was speaking in a state where he admittedly said he feels at home. Trump shouted that when a player demonstrates in such a manner the NFL owner should say "Get that SOB out of here!" As if that wasn't bad enough, Trump signified that the player should be poked with a blade with a twist inside his body. How sick is the man who holds the title President of the United States? An even greater question is how broken is the American political system? If the other two branches of government do not fulfill their Constitutional duties with speed and competence, the American dream could quickly turn into a nightmare for all.

ALABAMIANS IN POLITICAL HOSTAGE

On last Tuesday, Roy Moore won the Republican Primary Runoff in Alabama against Luther Strange. Strange was backed by Donald J. Trump and Mitch McConnell and the Republican establishment. Moore was supported by Steve Bannon and a rag tag team of white supremacists. Though Trump supported Strange he eagerly stated that if Strange lost he would back Moore. Moore will face Democratic opponent Doug Jones in the General Election in December. I am casually acquainted with Jones and know him to be a level headed, liberal and fair guy. However, for at least the last three decades, Alabama has been a very conservative state where very right-wing candidates have enjoyed success. So, Jones is in for the battle of his life. I wish him much success and hopefully his candidacy will signal an end to the political nightmare that has held Alabamians in political hostage for so long.

If Moore is successful then Alabama voters would have achieved the unthinkable feat of electing a candidate more extreme and despicable than Trump. God help America! If the devil exists Moore surely has met him and become his friend. Though it may appear strange that Moore has clothed himself in the Bible and especially the Ten Commandments because his messages and alleged behaviors are bone chilling demonic. Do not be surprised though the devil tempted Jesus Christ several times. If the Trump Administration and Congress were not already bound for Hell, with the appearance of Roy Moore in Washington, the devil would be there for the last leg of the voyage.

CARIBBEAN ISLANDS

Oh, how despicable is the person who sits in the White House? In the aftermath of the catastrophic storms that ravished the Caribbean Islands including Puerto Rico, Donald Trump has refused to devote his full attention to the citizens' survival and well-being, and to the territories full recovery. Trump chastised Mayor Carmen Cruz of San Juan for publically pleading for help and stating that the Island was not receiving the help it deserved. Trump's response was we got to figure out how to rebuild Puerto Rico and solve its debt problem. Excuse me Mr. President, Puerto Rico is in crisis. Rescue the people! Send food, clothing, shelter and medical aid and assistance. Get up off your ass and help these citizens. Devote full attention to these citizens as you did to the wealthy ones hit during a rash of hurricanes along the Gulf coast. The only differences in populations are one has more white citizens and wealth and the other has more people of color and less wealth. Has the US devolved back to a Colonial state of mind?

POLITICAL HYPOCRISY

It is simply not enough to call Donald Trump derogatory names. That is what he does best. If there are true public servants in Congress, then impeachment proceedings must commence at once. There was great fervor among Republicans to impeach the last two Democratic presidents. Where is that same outrage now especially in light of probable cause? Trumps sits with the smoking gun in his hand. What political hypocrisy? This president has surrounded himself with a cast of shady characters including family members who feed at the public trough and use the prestige and power of the US government for personal and private gain. How long will it take for all guilty individuals to be administered justice and removed from public office? In the Trump case, justice appears to be a bit tardy. As we teeter on the brink of war with an unconscionable president, all citizens and government officials must impeach this would be dictator and his minions. Lest we forget that the world waited too late on Hitler!

GOLD STAR FAMILY

Apparently, the tyrant in the White House cannot do anything right. This guy, Donald J. Trump, botched an attempt to console a Gold Star family. He called the widow of La David Johnson, a Green Beret, slain in combat mission recently in Niger, Africa with three of his comrades and stated "he knew what he was getting into but I guess it's sad anyway." Does this Trumpster have any human decency, respect or dignity? Trump's message was conveyed by Congresswomen Frederica Wilson and affirmed by Mrs. Johnson. Trump response was to demonize Congresswomen Wilson through several tweets by calling her wacky. He also insinuated that Mrs. Johnson's account of the embarrassing exchange was not accurate. I know it may be too late to potty-train a 70 something year old man but maybe this guy needs an adult sitter as implied by Senator Bob Corker in his reference to the White House as an adult daycare center. Maybe 24/7 care will help this president and keep him from harming himself and others. I would not be surprised at all if Trump is not put in a straight-jacket and placed in a padded cell before his tenure expires.

The word is that this guy ascended into office through a populist movement. So did fascism, Mussolini, Hitler and Franco!

Impeach him and lock him up! If Congress and or a majority of his Cabinet would come to their senses justice would prevail and the country would be spared of major blunders and disasters. If ever there was a time for God to bless America, it would be now.

REPUBLICAN DOMINATION

The Republicans dominate both Houses of Congress and have a sitting Republican president. Why both Houses choose to worship this president is beyond rationale. It just makes no sense. Trump has proven again and again that he disdains government, abhors the Constitutions, and acts as though he is above the law. He has little respect for anyone or anything except maybe his immediate family. Like a true narcissist, everything is always about him, his preferences, his emotions, his tweets and his lies. Only three Republican Senators to date have given Trump strong public condemnation for his un-presidential character and fitness. These three are John McCain, Bob Corker and Jeff Flake. Regardless of the specific reasons these politicians chose to break rank, their actions are good for the country and all of their colleagues should follow suit. Trump is rampaging through government like a bull in a china shop and teetering on the brink of World War III.

Trump is the only president in American history of which I am aware who lies at the drop of a hat by habit as if it's his favorite hobby. His avocation also includes bullying and belittling people. He is a supreme bully with a mental age of 10. Yet he claims to be "a very intelligent person who graduated from an Ivy League school." Strangely, I have not heard or read of any Ivy League college or university proudly claiming him as one of their most distinguished alumni.

The tyrant came to Washington with a band of malcontents, misfits and nincompoops to devolve government to enrich the rich and to wreak havoc on the masses. At every turn Trump appears to be enriching himself and family members and cronies through business holdings and deals. He promotes his properties on a regular basis by retreating to them for meetings, recreation and vacation.

12-DAY TRIP

Why are American taxpayers sponsoring a 12-day trip in the Pacific region for Trump and his entourage? Is this a personal business trip for Trump and his cronies? Or, is this a bona fide foreign policy trip? The answer lies in who benefits most: the American people or Trump's business interests and associates? Trump has demonstrated over and over again that he is first and foremost a businessman and not a public servant. Could it be that Trump surrounded himself with family members and business associates to procure business deals around the world for personal gain? I know that the Supreme Court cannot act on alleged presidential abuses of power until a case is brought before it. However, both Houses of Congress can proactively conduct investigations on alleged violations of the law by the president. A critical mass of sitting Congressional lawmakers are keenly aware of federal laws, corrupt practices and im-peachable offenses that may be filed against the president. Why these sworn officers of the US Congress do not act on behalf of the citizens of the nation? Some of these same Congressmen were overly eager to act with law suits, censures and impeach-ment procedures during recent democratic administrations but appear defenseless, reluctant, reticent and evasive during the appearance of a corrupt Republican regime.

COLLUSION WITH RUSSIA

At a time when it appears that all evidence points toward the Trump Administration and the Trump organization colluding with the Russian Empire to influence the 2016 Elections and to destabilize the American political system, the Republican dominated Congress willingly permits the would be tyrant and his minions to roam free. So as the Russian collusion case mounts against Trump and his administration, he takes a 12-day excursion of the Pacific. Bring Trump and his cronies to justice and confiscate all of their ill-gotten gains. Under the guise of a foreign policy trip, Trump and his cronies may be deceiving the American public.

JERUSALEM CAPITOL

The character in the White House with the wrecking ball announced on yesterday that the US recognizes Jerusalem as the Capitol of Israel. It's my understanding that Trump did not consult Congress or key Cabinet members before making this announcement. This is yet another example of tyrant like behavior. Maybe this action was intended to be a detraction from the onslaught of daily business and the looming FBI investigation of collusion and probable crimes with foreign parties. So, the president continues to trample along the global landscape creating havoc wherever he goes. What a compulsive and manic personality living in the White House? This person is without moral boundaries as evident by his admittedly grabbing and groping females, and his endorsement of an alleged pedophile, Roy Moore, seeking a Senate seat from Alabama. This detestable candidate was allegedly barred from an Alabama Mall for stalking teenage girls.

SEXUAL ABUSE SCANDALS

Two Democratic lawmakers caught up, in the rapidly growing sexual abuse scandals, John Conyers and Al Franken, resigned this week. They were more or less shamed and forced to resign by their Democratic colleagues. The Democrats seemingly choosing the high ground while the Republicans rush for cover. The President and other Republican scoundrels continue to deny countless sex abuse allegations against them, challenge accusers and refuse to step down from public office. If the Democrats were attempting to set a standard for Republicans to follow, I would wager 10:1 that their efforts would be in vain. This is a Republican party that is anti-people and lacking in moral standards as evident by their speech and actions.

SENATE RACE IN ALABAMA

The political climate in America is changing again. A Democrat, Doug Jones, won the Senate Race in Alabama. Democrats haven't won a statewide political race in Alabama in almost three decades. The last Democrat to win a statewide race was Donald Siegelman. Siegelman won the governor's race in 1998. I served in Siegelman's term of office as a Cabinet member. Granted Jones won the race against a most despicable candidate. A candidate who has been twice kicked off the Alabama Supreme Court; one accused several times of sexual assault on teenagers as young as 14 years old while in his early 30s; and allegedly barred from a Mall (shopping center) for stalking under age females. Jones won the election by a vote count of 673,896 (50%) to Moore's 651,972 (48 %). This close vote count indicates how tough it was for a Democrat to win a statewide race in Alabama. One former Alabama Democratic governor recently told me that he would run again for office when a Democrat could win in the state. So, over ½ million voters voted to send an accused pedophile to Washington over a law abiding and respectable Democrat. However as noted above the better angels in Alabama denounced him in favor of the Democrat. What explains this political phenomenon? Is it ignorance? Gullibility? Race? Policy or what? I would hypothe-size that all five are probable answers and contribute in important ways to this event.

Nevertheless, Alabama has sent a signal to America like Virginia, New Jersey and a few other states. The message is that the shameful Trump Administration and the Republican Party reign is nearing an end. The clear message is get the hell out of the way and let the Democrat run things again! The Republicans have proven to be morally deficient and predisposed toward corporate greed. Rather than serving the will of the people they are motivated to serve special interests at the expense of the American people. The head of the Republican Party, Donald J. Trump, is an admitted sex offender who gropes women and constantly speaks derogatorily toward females.

SHITHOLE COUNTRIES

Trump continues to produce evidence of a deceased mind and depraved heart. In a meeting on immigration with Senators on yesterday, Donald J. Trump asked why are we welcoming people from "shithole countries" like Haiti, Central America and Africa and not more from Norway? Of course, his point is the focus should be on welcoming white populations as oppose to populations of color. His inquiry was as racist as any of the Southern governors and other politicians who fought against advancements in civil rights for all Americans, or as hateful and disgraceful as any white supremacist or white nationalist who fought against the Abolition and Anti-slavery movement of the 19th Century. Trump's question is reprehensible, hateful, careless, detrimental, shameful and indefensible. While it may represent his true feelings about people of color, it does not represent America or the majority of Americans. This president must be constantly reminded that the majority of American voters did not cast their votes for him. In fact, a majority of the American electorates cast their votes for Hillary Clinton, his female opponent. I suppose that if Americans were given a choice of which of the US presidents should go to Hell, Trump's name would be at the top of the list. If Trump was put in a straight-jacket, strapped in a rocket and blasted one-way into space, the majority of Americans would cheer uncontrollably. This Trumpster has earned the title of the most reviled president in history. Trump's handlers should advise him to do more introspection. I assume that if he saw himself as others do, he would become more humble, civil and respectful toward others.

BAND OF MISFITS

Donald Trump and his band of misfits have allowed the US government to shutdown for failure to pass a budget. The Republican majority in Congress had little reservation in passing a tax reform bill that primarily benefitted the wealthy and major corporations. Yet this same political class would not provide funding for government to operate. This failure on behalf of the president and his Republican charlatans yet again act in ways to harm democratic institutions and citizens. Under the guise of an interest in immigration reform, the president and his Republican colleagues concocted a plan for DACA and CHIPS as incentives for democratic votes as parts of the funding bill. A primary goal was building a wall on the southern border of the US to prevent so called "illegal aliens" from entering the US. Just a few days ago Trump referred to "shithole countries" in reference to Central America. Even he is not dumb enough to understand that his immigration policy favored predominately white countries and especially white people as US immigration policy was prior to 1965. What will it take to reign in this tyrant? What will it take for the Republican leadership in Congress to regrow their spines and place checks and balances on the raving lunatic sitting in the Oval Office? This same group of Republicans routinely chased former President Barack Obama and Democratic leaders on alleged abuses and misconduct to no avail.

TRUMP BENEFICIARIES

Who are the true beneficiaries of Trump's doctrines and actions? Internationally, the beneficiaries are where Trump's business interests lay: Russia, Saudi Arabia, Philippines, and the leaders who serve his pleasures. Domestically, family members, Fortune 500 companies and their leaders and Republican leaders who enable, defend and support Trump's interests.

WHITE NATIONALISM

It appears that a major problem with the Trump Administration is that its primary goal is to create a white nation. In effect, the goal is to maintain white supremacy. From banning Muslims to "shithole countries", Trump's foreign and domestic policies are grounded in the false notion of superiority of the white race. This may be one of the principle reasons why Republicans enable and support him and his racist policies. The burden of proof should be placed upon the Trump Administration to prove that it's not a white supremacist establishment. Trump is a white nationalist!

25 BILLION DOLLARS WALL

Why would Congress authorize 25 billion dollars for Trump to build a wall on the southern border? Especially in light of his campaign slogan "Build the wall and Mexico will pay for it". No wall should be built nor should public money be spent to build it either. What impact would 25 billion dollars have on the provision of healthcare in America or on poverty in the US? Or, what effect would this amount of money have on the recovery and rebuilding of Puerto Rico and other Caribbean Islands in the aftermath of the devastating storms? Spending money on constructing a wall will not halt "illegal migration". It would line the pockets of the cronies who receive consulting and construction contracts for the political fiasco!

Don't authorize a dime for the racist policy. Why not treat people of color fairly who desire to immigrate to the US? Make immigration policy race, gender and religion neutral. There is nothing honorable about the Trump policy. Just follow the money of any contracts let associated with building a wall. If by hook or crook Congress authorizes money for a wall, a special prosecutor should be hired to oversee spending. I would not be surprised if laundered money from such a border wall project ended up in the bank accounts of the Trump organization and the accounts of his business associates. The president has proven himself to be corrupt and immoral.

SUFFER THE RUINS

How long must the world suffer the ruins of Donald J. Trump? Why does the Republican Congress enable him and his cronies? In 48 hours this feeble minded psycho president will stand before the nation and boldly state one lie after another. His speech will be flavored by assorted gossip and innuendoes. It will be his first State of the Union Address and hopefully his last. Unlike some who cannot stand to hear, see or read about him, I will watch and listen to his disgraceful, contentious and reprehensible rant. What a lousy and incorrigible character is Trump? If any individual or group of individuals should be barred from entry into America, it should be those of his ilk! No doubt Trump is one of the biggest mistakes and shams in US political history.

STATE OF THE UNION ADDRESS

I saw no person of color greeting the Donald as he walked into the Chamber. The President was surrounded by white males. The sucking through the nostrils sound was noticeable. Does he have an acute medical problem? The audience appeared to be almost totally white. My notes from the Trump address are below. None of his remarks were fact checked here. While these notes are not necessarily verbatim they capture the tone, tenor and syntax of Trumps' delivered remarks.

The state of our Union is strong because our people are strong. Together we can build a strong America. We are seeing rising wages. Unemployment claims have hit a 45 year low. Something I am proud of are African American and Hispanic unemployment rates being at their lowest in history. 401(k) and college pensions have gone through the roof. We have enacted the largest tax reform and cuts in American history. Nearly doubled the tax deduction for everyone. Doubled the child tax credit. Many families will have more take home pay starting next month. Repealed the core of Obamacare mandate.

We slashed the business tax rate from 35% to 21%. Small business will also receive a big tax break. More than 3 million workers have gotten bonuses since the tax cut. Apple plans to invest 350 billion dollars in the US. ExxonMobil plans to invest 50 billion dollars. We all share the American flag. We know faith and family are the values we share. In God we trust. We celebrate our military and veterans with unwavering support. We are totally defending our 2nd Amendment and protecting freedom of religion. We are giving choice in healthcare. We are restoring the VA and replacing people with those who love our veterans. Call our Congress to restore public trust and replace people who fail us. We have ended the war on energy. We have ended the war on beautiful clean coal. We have ended regulations on the Auto Industry in Detroit to get engines revving again. Now companies are roaring back to the US.

Last year the FDA approved more new drugs than ever in our country's history. We believe that patients with terminal illness should be treated with experimental drugs. They should have the right to try. One of our priorities is to reduce the price of prescription drugs. One of the top priorities for this year. Turned the page on unfair trade. Fair and reciprocal. Fix bad trade deals. Institute new ones. Rebuild crumbling infrastructure. America is a nation of builders. Safe, fast and modern that our people deserve. Asking Congress for 1.5 trillion dollars for infrastructure. We will build roads, bridges, railways and waterways across our land. Lift citizens from welfare to work; from poverty to prosperity. Invest in workforce development and job training. Let's open great vocational schools. Let's support working families by supporting family leave.

Reform prisons to give inmates a second chance at life. Reform immigration. Illegal immigrant gang members killing teenage African American girls. MS-13 Gang. Proposed legislation to fix our broken immigration laws. US is a compassionate nation. My greatest passion is for American children. Protect our children of every background, religion and creed. Protect the American dream because Americans are dreamers too. Congrats CJ for arresting 400 MS-13 Gang members in NYC. The government has incarcerated or sent thousands back to Mexico or back home. A path to citizenship to 1.8 million illegal immigrants brought to the country. A 12-year period for those who show good character and education. Secure the border-build a great wall on southern border. Close loopholes. End catch and release practice. End visa lottery. A merit based system. End chain migration. Limit to spouses and minor children. Time to reform and bring immigration into the 21st Century. Pledge to sign a bill that puts America first.

Reform will help opioid addiction. We must get tougher on drug dealers and pushers. Committed to fight the drug epidemic and get help to those who need it. We will prevail. We are restoring our strength abroad including China and Russia. End the Defense sequester and fully fund the military. We must modernize and rebuild our nuclear arsenal.

We pledged to defeat Isis. We are close to 100% elimination. We continue to work to eliminate Isis. Terrorists and unlawful combatants. I just signed an order directing Secretary Mattis to reexamine our detention polices and keep Guantanamo Bay. Our Army has new rules of engagement. No artificial guidelines and no longer tell enemies our plans. I authorize Jerusalem as our new Embassy in Israel. America stands with the people of Israel in their struggle. My Administration entered sanctions on Cuba and

Venezuela. North Korea- A menace that threatens our world. We are a people defending the American way. The people dreamed this country; made this country; and the people are making it great again. Thank you and God bless America.

REPUBLICAN MEMO

Devin Nunes and his fellow Republicans' memo was released several days ago. It was promoted by Trump supporters as proof that the FBI abused its surveillance powers through the procuring of FISA warrants; and that the FBI and DOJ were biased against Trump. After many days of hoopla regarding the damning content of the memo, it turns out that the charges in the memo appeared to be frivolous and wanting in substance. The memo was little more than rubbish.

Now Congressman Adam Schiff is seeking release of the Democrat response and rebuttal memo. The memo has been submitted to Trump for his approval for release. Even though there should be no question whether the memo should be released, I predict that Trump will not grant permission. Trump states that the Nunes memo clears him of any wrongdoing. Of course, the memo does not clear Trump of anything or anyone alleged in the Russian investigation. The Russian probe involves collusion with Russian interference in the 2016 Elections and possible obstruction of justice of the investigation by Trump and his associates. The Nunes memo was just another distraction from the Russian probe.

DEMOCRAT MEMO

Trump refuses to release Democrat response memo. His reasoning is that the memo reveals sources and methods and its length (10 pages). Trump states that the memo needs to be redacted and pass clearance. Ironically, Trump had no problem releasing the Republican memo even after being warned by FBI that the memo could cause grave harm regarding sources and methods. Either Trump assumes the public is dumb or he is the dumbest president ever to sit in the Oval Office.

It is quite amazing that the checks and balances system is very slow in halting the tyrannical behavior of Trump. The Republican dominated House and Senate continue to aid and abet Trump to the detriment of our democratic systems. Are the Republican leaders complicit in the Russian scandal? Have they cut Russian deals? Are they in collusion with Russia? Are they agents of Russia? The truth will come out eventually. It appears that the Mueller investigation, the Judiciary and the people are our saving grace. My hope is that justice will arrive sooner than later. The insatiable 10-year old in the White House wants a military parade. Yes, Donald J. Trump is pondering the parading of US military prowess. He was impressed by a French military parade while visiting President Macron of France. Well, he may have been impressed by France but I am certain that he was mindful of Kim Jong-un's frequent military parades. Why does this president have to be in a pissing contest with the world?

REMOVAL OF THE PRESIDENT

There are several lawful ways to remove a president from office in the US. The president may resign, be impeached or removed in accordance to the 25th Amendment or by death. Andrew Johnson was impeached in 1868; Richard Nixon was forced to resign in 1974; Bill Clinton was impeached in 1998 by the House but overruled by the Senate. Regrettably, several US presidents have been removed unlawfully by assassination including Abraham Lincoln in 1865, James Garfield in 1881, William McKinley in 1901 and John Kennedy in 1963. Imagine what path the country would have taken if they were fortunate enough to live out their terms.

SCHOOL SHOOTING

Another school shooting in America: this time in Florida at Stoneman Douglas High School. The shootings took the lives of 17 people (3 teachers and 14 students). As parents and students cry out for change to gun laws, the president's reply is arm teachers. The loss of one life is too many. How many more lives must be lost before the president and other politicians push back on NRA and its blood money? Until the situation changes, American families must prepare to bury more victims.

For those who say mental illness should be the main focus I reply that that is a copout! There has always been a significant portion of mental illness in the population. Mass shootings are at an all-time high. Could it be that we are selling more assault style weapons to anyone 18 or older without sufficient background checks? This kind of policy benefits most gun manufacturers, gun sellers and their vested interests as represented by NRA.

If elected officials do not change laws before the next election cycle, vote them out and elect those who will. America is the only advanced society with such a high frequency of school shootings and gun violence. Politicians who are wedded to NRA will not act in the public interests without constant prodding by their constituents.

The arming of teachers may create more problems than it solves. However, it would boost sales and profits for gun manufacturers and gun sellers. Why not start with common sense gun legislation? Enact laws that place restrictions on gun manufacturers, sellers and buyers. Laws that protect the public and increase safety for all citizens. Conduct full background checks. Don't sell guns to persons suffering from mental illness. Don't sell guns to violent criminals. Properly investigate gun threats. Bar guns from certain places except for licensed gun carriers, e.g. law enforcement personnel.

THE TYRANT IN THE WHITE HOUSE

Donald J. Trump: The tyrant in the White House. In his *Second Treatise of Government*, John Locke describes tyranny as the exercise of power beyond right…and making use of power…not for the good of those under it, but for his own private advantage. This Treatise was published in 1690. So, tyranny is not a new phenomenon in the world of politics. However, it is new in American politics. Never has there been a president in American history who possessed and coveted the persona and power of a tyrant until now. It appears that every thought and action of Mr. Trump are for his own personal gain and benefit. Suffice it to say that Trump is the first tyrant in the White House. Now it is time for the other two branches of government to reign him in and throw him out of office and into jail. Lock him up!

WORST PRESIDENT IN US HISTORY

Perhaps the worst president in US history has illuminated the imperfections of the checks and balances system. Here is a president who refuses to defend the national security of the US or its democratic institutions. One who refuses to follow or honor the rule of law. A person who doesn't seem to uphold the US Constitution. A president who may have committed high crimes and misdemeanors. One who rampages through the White House like a bull in a china shop. In light of all of these accusations of abuses of power, the Congress refuses to reign him in because of fear, cowardice or co-conspiracy. Congress has ability to act proactively and aggressively. The judiciary branch of government has authority to react. Until a matter is brought before the Supreme Court, it cannot act. So, if Congress doesn't reign in this tyrant then the people should act.

DEMOCRAT MEMO RELEASED

The Democrat memo in response to the Republican memo regarding the Russia Investigation was finally approved for release by Trump with redactions. Essentially, the Democrats purported to point out errors and omissions found in the Republican memo. In the final analysis, the Mueller investigation report is what really matters. Why Trump was eager to release the Republican memo and dragged his feet on releasing the Democrat memo is very suspicious. However suspicious though his behavior is consistent with past behavior of blocking and distorting information reflecting negatively on himself or contrary to his own beliefs and narratives. Mr. Trump is facing an uncertain future. After the Mueller investigation is completed, his options may become very limited and all of them may require him to vacate the Office of President. No one is above the law in the US. I can only envision that Trump will be found guilty of high crimes and misdemeanors related to his business dealings and his ties to Russia and other foreign countries and business associates.

EXECUTIVE BRANCH

Article II of the US Constitution applies to the Executive Branch. A section of Article II states that a president may be removed from office by death, resignation or inability to discharge the powers and duties of the office. So, on the occurrence of any of these events, the president ceases to occupy the office. Another section of Article II states that the president takes the following oath: "I do solemnly swear (or affirm) that I will faithfully execute the Office of President of the United States, and will to the best of my ability, preserve, protect and defend the Constitution of the United States." Can it be declared that Donald J. Trump was true to this oath? In Section 4 of Article II, it states "The President, Vice President and all civil officers of the United States, shall be removed from office on Impeachment for and conviction of Treason, Bribery or other high crimes and misdemeanors." Is Donald J. Trump guilty of any of these offenses? Amendment 25 provides for the removal of the President upon written notice of the Vice President and a majority of either the principal officers of the Executive Departments or of such other body as Congress may by law provide declaring that the president is unable to discharge the powers and duties of his office. Is Donald J. Trump able to discharge his presidential powers and duties?

BEYOND TRUMP

Most citizens of goodwill welcome the departure of Trump and his Administration. As the majority of voters who cast votes in the 2016 Elections knew of his unfitness to serve now pray for his speedy removal. In the US system of justice, a person is presumed innocent until proven guilty. It appears imminent that Trump and persons associated with his regime will be proven guilty of high crimes and misdemeanors. For American citizens, the Russian investigation cannot come to an end too soon. I truly believe that if the investigation concludes that Trump and his associates are innocent of any alleged crimes that they should be left alone. However, if the investigation finds Trump and his associates guilty of any crime, then justice should be swift and appropriate for the crime or crimes. If the latter is the case, the indicted individuals should be immediately removed from office and incarcerated awaiting conviction and adjudication. If Trump is removed from office, a new president should take office in accordance to the US Constitution. The new president should immediately begin restoring America's integrity and reestablishing faith and support for democratic institutions. Lessons should be learned from the

Trump regime especially how a tyrannical president challenges our system of checks and balances.

PRESIDENT-ELECT EXAMINATION

Trump's presidency raises the question of whether the president-elect should be thoroughly examined before taking office. The broader question is should the president-elect be held to a higher standard than other elected officials of Congress? I believe the Trump experience makes the case in the affirmative. The examination or examinations that I have in mind involve (s) character and fitness, intelligence and competence, and physical stamina and emotional stability. While I am prone to believe that such exams would be undemocratic, I believe in cases like Trump's, the greater public good would be served. The results would become the determining factor as to whether the president-elect would be sworn into office. However, realizing that we are dealing with human beings and not angels, it may be best to require the exam(s) and use the results for information purposes only. The results should be released to the public in any case.

CONCLUSION

Trump and his Administration have tested the American political system especially the rule of law, the Constitution and the checks and balances. If justice prevails and I believe it will, American democracy and the American spirit will reign again from sea to shining sea. I still have faith in the better angels of America and hope in our democratic systems. America has come through the Colonial Period, the Revolution, Slavery and the Abolition movement, the Civil War, Jim Crow and Segregation, the Populist Movement, World I and II, the Korean War, the Civil Rights Movement, the Viet Nam War, the Student Movement, the Women's Movement, Gay and Lesbian Movement, War on Terrorism, Occupy Wall Street, Black Lives Matter, Me Too and the current Student Movement. I predict that Trump will not finish his first term. Political order will be restored in America. Democrats will reign again in 2020 and 2024. So, there is hope in America beyond Trump. God will bless America!

www.ingramcontent.com/pod-product-compliance
Lightning Source LLC
Chambersburg PA
CBHW070042260726
48658CB00002B/688